The Nicest Time of Year

The Nicest Time of Year

WRITTEN AND ILLUSTRATED BY ZHENYA GAY

THE VIKING PRESS · NEW YORK

To M. M.
for her birthday at
"the nicest time of year"

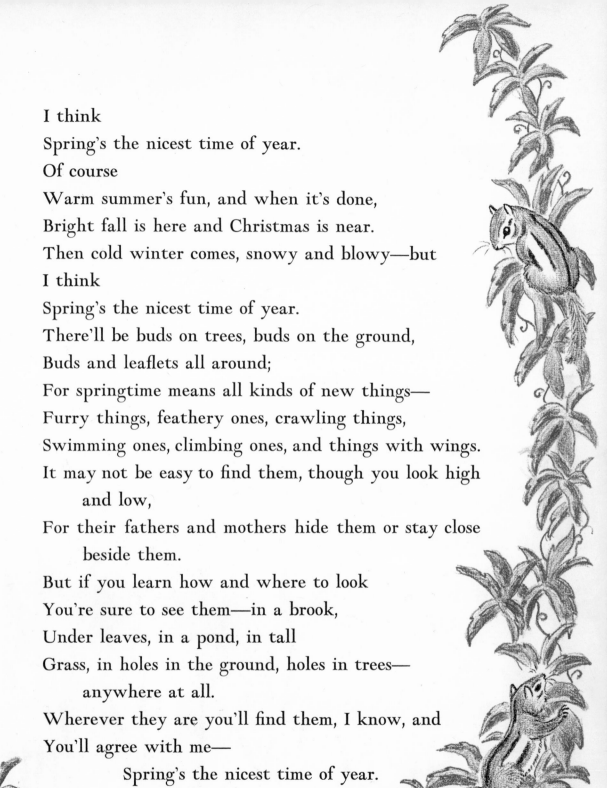

I think
Spring's the nicest time of year.
Of course
Warm summer's fun, and when it's done,
Bright fall is here and Christmas is near.
Then cold winter comes, snowy and blowy—but
I think
Spring's the nicest time of year.
There'll be buds on trees, buds on the ground,
Buds and leaflets all around;
For springtime means all kinds of new things—
Furry things, feathery ones, crawling things,
Swimming ones, climbing ones, and things with wings.
It may not be easy to find them, though you look high
    and low,
For their fathers and mothers hide them or stay close
    beside them.
But if you learn how and where to look
You're sure to see them—in a brook,
Under leaves, in a pond, in tall
Grass, in holes in the ground, holes in trees—
    anywhere at all.
Wherever they are you'll find them, I know, and
You'll agree with me—
        Spring's the nicest time of year.

In springtime get up early in the morning. Go for a
walk with a grown-up friend. When you see brown
leaves from wintertime on the ground, walk slowly,
go softly, stop and peek under the leaves. You may find

BABY RABBITS

When you come to bushes that make shadows in the sunlight, move quietly and slowly, look closely. You may find that a mother deer has hidden her

FAWNS

When you walk through tall grass, go carefully and watch closely. You may find a nest of

BABY BIRDS

When you see a SMALL hole in the ground, sit down near it and wait quietly. Out of the small hole may come

BABY CHIPMUNKS

When you see a BIG hole in the ground, sit down near it and wait quietly too. You may be the first to see

BABY WOODCHUCKS

At noon, when the sun is high in the sky, start on your way home. Look up into the trees. On a branch safe and high you may see a mother

OPOSSUM *and her* BABIES

For lunch, eat a sandwich and drink a glass of cool milk. Take a nap. Wake up and read a book or play a game with other boys and girls. In late afternoon, when the sun is low in the sky, go for another walk with your grown-up friend. When you come to an old hollow tree, find a comfortable place and sit down on the ground. Stay there patiently and watch. You may see

FLYING SQUIRRELS, *that live in old hollow trees*

When you get up and go on your way, walk quietly.
You may get a glimpse of

RACCOONS *fishing at the edge of a brook*

As the sun is setting, start toward home, but stop for
a little while when you come to a pond. Get way
down on your hands and knees and look into the water
and watch tiny, black

TADPOLES

On your way home, look closely at old stone walls. Where the sun has warmed the stones all day long you may see a beautiful

BLACK SNAKE

25

Ask your grown-up friend to lift you high so you can look over the stone wall to the meadow on the other side. You may see small black and white figures moving one after another through the grass. That will be a parade of

BABY SKUNKS *and their mother out for a walk too*

When you reach home, say thank you and good-by to your grown-up friend. Eat your dinner and enjoy it. But, just before you go to bed, look out-of-doors. You'll probably see a

WHIPPOORWILL *crouched low to the ground,*
singing his song under the stars and the moon

Now go to bed. Spring sounds will sing you to sleep: the whippoorwill's cry, the owl's hoot, and a merry chorus of frog song. And you'll dream of all you've seen today and will see again tomorrow, and the next day, and the next, all through springtime, the nicest time of year!

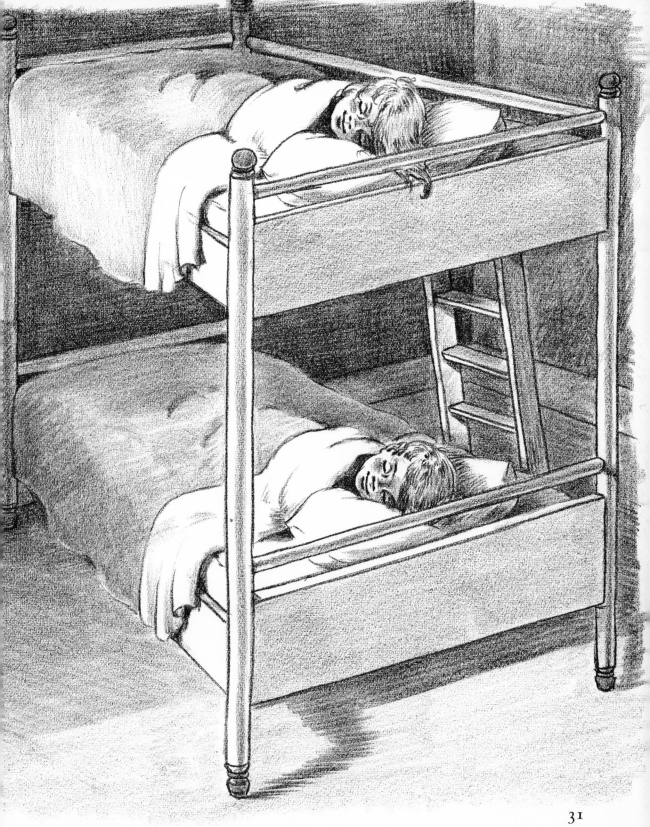

MAPLE SCHOOL

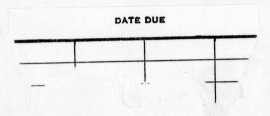

DATE DUE